Cognitive Behavioral Therapy

Treat Any Addiction - Kick Any Habits

James Stafford

Disclaimer

This document is geared towards providing exact and reliable information in regards to the topic and issue covered. The publication is sold with the idea that the publisher is not required to render accounting, officially permitted, or otherwise, qualified services. If advice is necessary, legal or professional, a practiced individual in the profession should be ordered. In no way is it legal to reproduce, duplicate, or transmit any part of this document in either electronic means or in printed format. Recording of this publication is strictly prohibited and any storage of this document is not allowed unless with written permission from the publisher. All rights reserved. The information provided herein is stated to be truthful and consistent, in that any liability, in terms of inattention or otherwise, by any usage or abuse of any policies, processes, or directions contained within is the solitary and utter responsibility of the recipient reader. Under no circumstances will any legal responsibility or blame be held against the publisher for any reparation, damages, or monetary loss due to the information herein, either directly or indirectly. The information herein is offered for informational purposes solely, and is universal as so. The presentation of the information is without contract or any type of guarantee assurance. This book is not intended for use as a source of legal, medical, business, accounting or financial advice. All readers are advised to seek services of competent professionals in the legal, medical, business, accounting, and finance fields.

Table of Contents

Chapter I

What Is Cognitive Behavioral Therapy?

What Is CBT?

If you have recently started therapy or have been considering treatment for drug abuse, you're likely to hear about cognitive behavioral therapy (CBT).

CBT is an approach to treatment that was originally developed to treat depression but has been expanded to improve symptoms of various mental health illnesses and issues including:

* Addiction.
* Anxiety.
* Psychosis.
* Trauma.

A major component of CBT is that thoughts, feelings and behaviors are connected in a way that one influences and is influenced by the others. For example: feelings are impacted by your thoughts and behaviors.

So, if you have feelings that you do not like, you can modify them by changing your thoughts and behaviors.

What CBT Is Not

Cognitive behavioral therapy should not be confused with the following:
* Psychoanalysis - This Freudian approach aims to get at the bottom of subconscious determinants of your actions/behavior.

* Person-centered/ humanistic therapy - This approach involves a mostly-passive therapist that says little during sessions in an attempt to have you resolve your issues independently.

How Does CBT Aid in Addiction Recovery?

The goal of CBT is to increase your awareness of your thoughts, actions and the consequences of each. Through this process, you gain a better understanding of your motivations and the role of drug abuse in your life.

Cognitive Distortions

Many times, cognitive behavioral therapy will focus on studying your thought patterns to look for negative views of yourself, the world around you and your future. Chances are good that there will be flawed perceptions called cognitive distortions.
These distortions are like a dark lens that changes the way you view the world. Some cognitive distortions include:

* All-or-nothing thinking: Perceiving situations in absolute, black-and-white categories.

* Overgeneralization: Viewing a recent, negative event as a never-ending pattern of defeat.

* Mental filter: Dwelling only on the negatives.

* Disqualifying the positive: Insisting that your positives don't count because of some other force.
* Jumping to conclusions: Assuming your thoughts, feelings or beliefs are true without any supporting evidence.

By changing your thoughts to become more positive, you can improve your feelings and behaviors.

Co-occurring Disorders

CBT will also prove helpful in identifying and treating comorbid mental health issues that often accompany addiction. Many people engage in addictive behaviors to escape or avoid emotional pain.

CBT can address those psychological issues directly to:

* Reduce the underlying reasons for addiction.
* Prevent future relapse.

What Should I Expect in CBT?

CBT helps clients learn skills that can be used in the present and interventions that can be applied to the future to reduce stress, improve behaviors and increase overall well-being.

CBT will look very different depending on the therapist and the setting. A strong benefit of CBT is that it allows for incredible flexibility and freedom. Generally, your therapist will serve several functions during the course of your treatment:

* Teacher. She will provide education regarding your symptoms, diagnosis and treatment. (Homework may be given to gather more information away from session.)

* Teammate. As you work through the process, she will assist with your follow-through on planned interventions to achieve your goals.

A typical CBT session will last 45 minutes to an hour and will involve discussing irrational thoughts, negative behaviors, and stress of the last week. From there, your therapist will challenge your negative thinking and faulty beliefs while offering positive coping skills to employ when faced with challenges.

CBT helps clients learn skills that can be used in the present and interventions that can be applied to the future to reduce stress, improve behaviors and increase overall well-being.

CBT WORKS

Simply, CBT is a frequently used therapeutic style for addiction and mental illness because it works. In fact, CBT has been studied and tested over the years to prove its efficacy and value in a number of settings and for a number of presenting problems.

Other CBT Techniques

Other interventions in CBT include:

* Relaxation training for anxiety.
* Assertiveness training to improve relationships.
* Self-monitoring education to improve insight.
* Cognitive restructuring to modify thinking patterns.

Finding Addiction Treatment that Includes CBT

If you are interested in starting cognitive behavioral therapy, you are in luck. Because of its strong reputation for being effective across a range of issues, mental health professionals trained in CBT are widely available. Chances are high that any outpatient individual, outpatient group, inpatient, residential treatment or rehabilitation program you would attend will be staffed with competent CBT therapists.

The best news is that CBT is very low-risk. The odds of something negative or harmful happening from attending a CBT session is minimal. The reward is a different matter.

If you are not convinced that addiction, depression, anxiety or other issues are negatively impacting your life, a CBT therapist can assess your situation and symptoms to see if you meet criteria for a mental health diagnosis. CBT therapists work with people looking to achieve more from life, as well as people with serious mental health and substance use issues.

Other Supplemental Therapies

Another major benefit of CBT is that it integrates aspects of other styles well while allowing clients to benefit from other services. Many CBT therapists utilize aspects of the following orientations into their sessions:

* Motivational Interviewing - This style
of therapy involves a certain method of
questioning that is particularly helpful in
addiction, and it fits easily with CBT.

* Holistic Approach - A holistic approach
will look at your overall well-being to find
ways to improve your physical, emotional
and spiritual health.

* 12-Step Programs - Some differences of
opinion exist between programs like AA
and NA, but the similarities are enough to
make these two interventions work well
together. Many clients will attend regular
meetings in conjunction with their CBT
sessions.

* Medication Management - When you
work with a CBT therapist, they might
recommend a psychiatric evaluation. You
may be prescribed medication to help
improve your symptoms. Many studies
show that CBT and medication work
better together than either alone.

Chapter II

Cognitive Behavior Therapy for Addiction

Cognitive behavior therapy (CBT) is commonly used to treat depression, anxiety disorders, phobias, and other mental disorders. Yet, it has also been shown to be valuable in treating alcoholism and drug addiction. This is especially true when it's part of an overall program of recovery.

Cognitive-behavioral coping skills treatment is a short-term, focused therapeutic approach to helping drug-dependent people become abstinent.

It does so by using the same learning processes you used to develop alcohol and drug dependence in the first place.

Cognitive behavior therapy is based on the idea that feelings and behaviors are caused by a person's thoughts, not on outside stimuli like people, situations, and events. While you may not be able to change your circumstances, you can change how you think about them. According to cognitive behavior therapists, this helps you change how you feel and behave.

In the treatment for alcohol and drug dependence, the goal of CBT is to:

* Teach the person to recognize situations in which they are most likely to drink or use drugs.

* Avoid these circumstances if possible.
* Cope with other problems and behaviors which may lead to their substance abuse.

What Are Other Approaches to CBT?

According to the National Association of Cognitive-Behavioral Therapists, there are several approaches to CBT.

This includes Rational Emotive Behavior Therapy, Rational Behavior Therapy, Rational Living Therapy, Cognitive Therapy, and Dialectic Behavior Therapy.

What Are the Components of CBT?

In its use to treat alcohol and drug dependent individuals, CBT has two main components: functional analysis and skills training.

Functional Analysis: Working together, the therapist and individual try to identify the thoughts, feelings, and circumstances that led to and followed drinking or using. This helps determine the risks that are likely to lead to a relapse.

Functional analysis can also give insight into why they drink or use drugs in the first place. This helps identify situations in which the person has coping difficulties.

Skills Training: If someone is at the point where they need professional treatment for their addiction, chances are they are using alcohol or drugs as their main means of coping with problems. The goal of CBT is to get the person to learn or relearn better-coping skills.

The therapist tries to help the individual unlearn old habits and learn to develop healthier skills and habits. The main goal is to educate them about ways to change how they think about their substance abuse. Then they can learn new ways to cope with the situations and circumstances that led to their drinking or drugging episodes in the past.

How Long Does CBT Take?

Because cognitive behavior therapy is a structured, goal-oriented educational process focused on immediate problems, the process is usually short-term. Although other forms of therapy and psychoanalysis can take years, CBT is usually completed in 12 to 16 sessions with the therapist.

How Effective Is Cognitive Behavior Therapy?

According to the National Institute on Drug Abuse, more than 24 randomized controlled trials have been conducted among users of tobacco, alcohol, cocaine, marijuana, opiates, and other types of substances. This makes cognitive-behavioral treatments one of the most frequently evaluated psychosocial approaches to treating substance use disorders.

In these studies, CBT has been shown most effective when compared with having no other treatment at all. When compared with other treatment approaches, studies have had mixed results. Some show CBT to be more effective while others show it to be of equal, but not greater, effectiveness than other treatments.

As with other treatments for alcoholism and drug abuse, including pharmaceutical treatments, cognitive behavior therapy works best when combined with other recovery efforts. This includes participation in support groups like Alcoholics Anonymous or Narcotics Anonymous.

In short, behavior cognitive therapy works well for some, but not for everyone. This is the case with all alcoholism and drug treatment approaches because every person deals with and recovers from addiction in a different way.

Cognitive Behavioral Therapy and Drug Addiction

As an Alternative Treatment for Addiction, Cognitive Behavioral Therapy is Proving to Increase the Chances of Long-Term Sobriety

If you are seeking a non-NA alternative drug recovery program, chances are that you have heard the phrase 'Cognitive Behavioral Therapy' (CBT) before. This part of the non-twelve step recovery effort focuses on the notion that overcoming dependence and maintaining long-term sobriety is about more than just 'going cold turkey,' it is about being able to say goodbye to unhealthy behaviors and moving on without relying on illicit substances to bring about positive changes.

Understanding the Issue

CBT is about understanding and providing insights as to why a person abuses drugs or alcohol in the first place. What is it that drives the compulsion? The physical dependence on illicit substances is not the 'problem,' but rather a serious issue resulting from the constant underlying needs.

It is possible to have a patient undergo withdrawal and be completely physically independent from drugs or alcohol, but unless there are strategies in place to ensure that the patient stays sober in the future, a relapse is likely. Simply put, patients have to understand how to replace their addictive behaviors with a positive alternative.

Before you can understand why so many non-AA or non-NA programs advocate CBT, you have to understand what it is. It is a form of psychotherapy.

According to the definition from the National Association of Cognitive Behavioral Therapists (NACBT), this form of therapy emphasizes the importance of thinking about what we do and how we feel. CBT is a relatively short-term, focused approach that helps users understand and recognize specific situations in which they are prone to engage in addictive behaviors.

It is interesting to note that CBT is not a distinct therapeutic technique that can easily be identified. Rather, it is a general term for a classification for a number of similar therapies. These different therapies include Dialectic Behavior Therapy, Rational Living Therapy, Rational Emotive Behavior Therapy, Cognitive Therapy, and Rational Behavior Therapy. When used as a part of an overall recovery program, it has proven extremely promising.

Further Explanation of the Key Components of CBT

As earlier discussed in this book, Cognitive Behavioral Therapy has two key components: skills training and functional analysis. We look at both of them in a bit more detail:

Functional analysis – Both the therapist and the patient work together to identify circumstances, thoughts and feelings that the patient experiences before and after he or she uses illicit substances.

This will help the patient understand risky behaviors and choices that may potentially lead to a relapse. Especially during the early treatment phase, this functional analysis is critical. Not only will it identify potential triggers, but also allows patients to understand and avoid high-risk situations. It also provides insights as to why the patient turns to drugs or alcohol in the first place. Is it because of achieving euphoria not otherwise available?

Is it about escaping from reality? Perhaps it is about coping with interpersonal difficulties. Regardless
of the trigger, it is important that both parties come to an understanding of the issue.

Skills training – This is the step where the patient will begin to unlearn old destructive habits and come up with new and healthier ways to replace these old habits. The reasons that a patient may have turned to drugs to deal with intrapersonal or interpersonal issues may include:

* Never having learned effective strategies to deal with challenges that people face in their adult life. Especially those who started substance abuse early (during adolescence) often have no healthy ideas how to deal with problems.

* Chronic involvement in a drug-using lifestyle. Even if the user once had effective strategies to deal with stress and challenges at one point, the constant drug seeking, drug using and periods of recovering from use, may have replaced any other effective coping mechanism.

* Drug abuse and other problems may have weakened the ability to use effective strategies that the patient may have learned in the past.

Relevant Features of Cognitive Behavioral Therapy

There are a number of important factors that have to be taken into consideration before using CBT. These are a few of the key components:

* It is short-term – Successful alternative drug recovery programs do not talk about recovery in weeks, but rather in months and years. However, CBT has a specific point where the formal therapy is going to end, meaning it is time-limited. This is not a never-ending treatment approach.

* It is effective – Because CBT is effective within this relatively short period of time, it is an attractive approach for alternative treatments to consider. There is solid empirical support and rigorous clinical trials that have proven it to be effective.

* It is structured and directive – Once every session begins, there is a specific agenda and specific concepts or techniques that are used during every session. The focus of Cognitive Behavioral Therapy is what the client wants, not what the therapist believes that the client's goals should be.The person struggling with dependence reveals his or her goals to the therapist and the CBT

therapist directs the patient in such a way that they can attain those goals.

* It is inherently flexible – Flexibility plays a key component in Cognitive Behavioral Therapy. Even though results are positive in conjunction with long-term, inpatient recovery programs, its effectiveness works with either individual or group sessions. Even outpatient programs may benefit from it.

* A collaborative effort – This is not a method that only requires passive participation from one of the two participants. The patient needs to share what he or she wants and the therapist will assist in achieving those goals. The patient expresses concerns, learns and implements. Meanwhile, the therapist listens, teachers and encourages.

* Based on an educational model – CBT is based on the notion that the vast majority of our emotional and behavioral reactions are learned. The goal is to identify maladaptive behavior, unlearn it

and come up with an alternative method of reacting to certain triggers, which proves healthier in the future. Because of the educational component, even with a short- term program, it can lead to long-term results. This is about understanding what needs to change in order to seek the desired outcome in the future.

Cognitive Behavioral Therapy is an evidence-based form of therapy. It helps the patient identify and unlearn addictive behavior and replace this with healthier behavior that puts them on the path towards recovery. Learn more about how the various methodologies of Cognitive Behavioral Therapy are applied to drug and alcohol rehabilitation, and what it can do for you.

Chapter III
Cognitive Behavioral Therapy and Medications

If you have an anxiety disorder, a basic question that you may ask yourself is: "How do I get better?" If you happen to bring this up to your doctor, they are very likely to prescribe you a drug without even mentioning the most effective, scientifically validated treatment around: Cognitive Behavioral Therapy or CBT for short.

Over the past 20 or 30 years or so, scientists have discovered several principles that help people overcome their fears. These principles have to do with how thinking affects or colors emotional responses and how specific behaviors contribute either to helpful and adaptive emotional responses or painful and difficult ones.

These principles contributed to the formation of a new type of therapy called Cognitive-Behavioral Therapy.

The Cognitive part (which means thinking) works by teaching people to change harmful, overly fearful, and non-realistic anxious thinking into more positive and realistic ways of thinking. The underlying assumption is: If you change the way you think, you will change the way you feel.

The Behavioral part works by teaching people to engage in behaviors that have a calming effect to reduce anxious arousal, and by learning new behavior to face, rather than avoid fears through a process of Therapeutic Exposure to the fears.

Cognitive Behavioral approaches for Anxiety Disorders are superior to medication in reducing anxiety and preventing relapse. Still most Americans have rarely heard of it and since many medical doctors do not have ready access to this approach, medication is often prescribed for anxiety disorders.

Lets take a look at the major classes of drugs used to "treat" anxiety disorders. There are two main classes of medication most commonly prescribed to treat anxiety: Tranquilizers (a class or grouping of Benzodiazepine based medicines like Xanax, Ativan, and Valium) and anti-depressants (like Prozac, Paxil, Zoloft, and Welbutrin). There are many, many more as well.

The most recent research suggests that while Benzodiazepine medications work faster, there are many problems associated with their usage (including addiction and anxiety rebound when they are discontinued). The plain truth is that drugs are also associated with a variety of unpleasant side effects: weight gain, sexual dysfunction (like difficulty achieving orgasm and loss of desire), dry mouth, headaches, gastrointestinal distress and many others.

Weight gain and sexual dysfunction are particularly common. Another significant problem with all classes of drug treatment for anxiety disorders is that once the drug is removed, the chances of a relapse are much greater than after a successful course of Cognitive Behavioral Therapy.

The simple truth is that drugs only work while you take them! If you learn specific coping skills through CBT, they become a part of you for the rest of your life resulting in significantly reduced anxiety even after treatment has ended.

Cognitive Behavioral approaches to emotional problems, have been shown repeatedly by rigorous scientific studies to significantly reduce panic, anxiety, worry, and fear in a variety of well controlled studies. It has now been demonstrated that for certain Anxiety Disorders (including Panic Disorder and Agoraphobia), that these approaches have better outcomes and far less relapse then medication (again, when you go off the drug, the symptoms at some point usually come back). Most people are unaware of these findings because medication is by far still the most common treatment for anxiety problems.

Unfortunately, per above, medication does not teach skills! Brain imaging studies have shown that after people underwent a course of Cognitive Behavioral Therapy they experienced a decrease in the fear center of the brain!

Chapter IIII
Couples Drug Therapy: Is it the Solution to Drug and Alcohol Addiction?

Cognitive Behavioral Therapy is a cornerstone of the therapeutic treatment of addiction. Couples drug treatment is an excellent example of successful behavioral therapy.

Couples drug therapy has proven to be the most effective method of treating substance abuse in the family therapy setting. In 1974, the National Institute on Alcohol Abuse and Alcoholism praised couples therapy and family therapy for outstanding advances in the treatment of addiction.

In behavioral therapy, the individual seeking help takes an active role. In couples drug therapy, there is a greater opportunity for a successful outcome using the support of the involved partner. As both partner's behaviors are intertwined, there is an interaction in their personalities, substance abuse issues, moods,and anxieties. As a result, addiction treatment is most successful when addicted couples support one another during recovery.

Cognitive Behavior Therapy (CBT) is a psychotherapeutic approach that focuses on resolving dysfunctional behaviors, thought processes and emotions using a systematic, goal-oriented process.

Much empirical evidence exists that supports the effectiveness of CBT in treating a variety of disorders. Couples drug therapy has shown impressive results using this technique-driven approach. Success comes from using the strong connection between the partners to encourage certain behaviors through positive reinforcement.

It has been shown that both men and women achieve meaningful recovery using this technique of mutual support, although there are somewhat higher success rates for women.

Couples alcohol treatment also addresses the life changes that will occur for both partners as a result of CBT. Strategies for continuing positive reinforcement are developed that anchor the relationship in corrective replacement behaviors. The couple then has the tools needed for a healthy relationship.

There is far more to a successful outcome in substance abuse treatment than simply ending the cycle of addiction. It must be recognized that there are behaviors that existed before and will continue to exist after active addiction that will need to be addressed.

These behaviors have an impact on the couple's interaction that can lead to relapse if no change occurs.

In couples drug therapy, this change is crucial to avoid slipping back into the addiction cycle for the emotional release that drugs and alcohol provide. Unfortunately, the alcohol merely masks the difficulties temporarily. Couples drug treatment allows these necessary changes to occur in a safe environment.

In addition, both partners are encouraged to become engaged in support programs to facilitate their individual recovery. There they learn about challenges that are commonly faced by couples. Al-Anon is a very supportive program that has existed for 60 years.

It encourages fellowship among relatives and friends of the alcoholic. Through sharing experiences, members receive strength, support and information necessary for recovery.

Couples drug therapy is often the key to the recovery of the addict. It takes into account the dynamics of all of the relationships affected by the addiction. As a result, life partners and family members can enjoy the recovery of the addict, while learning new skills that strengthen the

family relationship. Successful treatment
results in a stronger bond which honors
the original love and devotion that
brought the partners together.

Chapter V
Cognitive Behavioral Therapy for Addiction works real good

Drug addiction is a progressive neurological disease which requires clinical treatment. The only way for addicts to achieve long-term sobriety is through holistic treatment programs which address the physiological, mental, and spiritual aspects of addiction.

Some of the most proven techniques for treating addiction are known as "evidence-based therapies" because of their rigorous testing and government approval. These methods include individual counseling sessions, group therapy, and family therapy. Overall, these therapies are designed to teach addicts coping mechanisms for dealing with future cravings.

However, many rehabilitation clinics across the United States use other highly-successful treatment methods. For treating the mental problems associated with addiction, clinicians often employ cognitive-behavioral therapy.

This type of therapy teaches addicts that their emotions and behaviors are controlled by their thoughts - and thus well within their control while sober. This is hugely important for addicts, as control issues are often what lead to drug use in the first place.

There are two main components of cognitive-behavioral therapy: analysis and response training. During the analysis phase of this therapy, clinicians help patients discover some of the root causes of their drug use and addictions. Addicts learn to recognize the thoughts and feelings they experience when they crave drugs.

For example, some alcoholics may come to realize that they impulsively drink whenever they become nervous or frightened.

On the other hand, people addicted to cocaine, meth, or other stimulants may find that high workloads and feelings of anxiety drive them to use drugs.

Overall, learning about these drug-associated feelings is crucial for addicts to develop effective mechanisms for dealing with cravings. By identifying dangerous emotions, they can then learn to think through their
problems and alter their mental states in healthier ways.

Addicts learn these coping mechanisms during response training. After identifying the emotions which trigger their drug use, patients learn healthy ways to proactively prevent negative feelings and react productively when they occur.

For instance, people who typically use marijuana when stressed might learn to instead deal with their stress through meditation or objective analysis of their problems.

 They might also learn to avoid stressors in the first place by analyzing the areas in their life which most often lead to depressive thoughts and feelings. Negative relationships, co-occurring mental illnesses, and financial difficulties are problems which addicts can address during cognitive behavioral therapy.

Like most other addiction treatment methods - and like the disease of addiction itself - cognitive behavioral therapy is progressive. It requires consistent effort from rehab patients and clinicians alike and is typically just one component of many in a comprehensive treatment program.

Although residential inpatient programs are the most involved and most effective at treating severe cases of addiction, patients can receive this therapy during partial hospitalization and outpatient treatment, as well.
Whatever your situation is, help is available now. If you or someone you know is struggling with addiction, follow the links below for a toll-free, no-obligation consultation. Our dedicated

addiction specialists will help you find a treatment plan that fits your budget, your life, and your specific drug problems. Don't wait until it's too late - get help today.

Chapter VI
What Constitutes Cognitive Behavioral Therapy?

Cognitive behavioral therapy is a psychotherapeutic approach that aims to teach a person new skills on how to solve problems concerning dysfunctional emotions, behaviors, and cognitions through a goal-oriented, systematic approach.

This title is used in many ways to differentiate behavioral therapy, cognitive therapy, and therapy that is based on both behavioral and cognitive therapies. There is empirical evidence that shows that cognitive behavioral therapy is quite effective in treating several conditions, including personality, anxiety, mood, eating, substance abuse, and psychotic disorders.

Treatment is often manualized, as specific psychological orders are treated with specific technique-driven brief, direct, and time-limited treatments.

Cognitive behavioral therapy can be used both with individuals and in groups. The techniques are often adapted for self-help sessions as well. It is up to the individual clinician or researcher on whether he/she is more cognitive oriented, more behavioral oriented, or a combination of both, as all three methods are used today.

Cognitive behavioral therapy was born out of a combination of behavioral therapy and cognitive therapy. These two therapies have many differences, but found common ground on focusing on the "here and now" and on alleviating symptoms.

Evaluating cognitive behavioral therapy has led to many believing that it is more effective over psychodynamic treatments and other methods.

The United Kingdom advocates the use of cognitive behavioral therapy over other methods for many mental health difficulties, including post-traumatic stress disorder, obsessive-compulsive disorder, bulimia nervosa, clinical depression, and the neurological condition chronic fatigue syndrome/ myalgic encephalomyelitis.

The precursors of cognitive behavioral therapy base their roots in various ancient philosophical traditions, especially Stoicism. The modern roots of CBT can be traced to the development of behavioral therapy in the 1920s, the development of cognitive therapy in the 1960s, and the subsequent merging of the two therapies.

The first behavioral therapeutic approaches were published in 1924 by Mary Cover Jones, whose work dealt with the unlearning of fears in children.

The early behavioral approaches worked well with many of the neurotic disorders, but not so much with depression. Behavioral therapy was also losing in popularity due to the "cognitive revolution." This eventually led to cognitive therapy being founded by Aaron T. Beck in the 1960s.

The first form of cognitive behavioral therapy was developed by Arnold A. Lazarus during the time period of the late 1950s through the 1970s. During the 1980s and 1990s, cognitive and behavioral therapies were combined by work done by David M. Clark in the United Kingdom and David H. Barlow in the United States.

Cognitive behavioral therapy includes the following systems: cognitive therapy, rational emotive behavior therapy, and multimodal therapy. One of the greatest challenges is defining exactly what a cognitive-behavioral therapy is. The particular therapeutic techniques vary within the different approaches of CBT depending upon what kind of problem issues are being dealt with, but the techniques usually center around the following:

- Keeping a diary of significant events and associated feelings, thoughts, and behaviors.

- Questioning and testing cognitions, evaluations, assumptions, and beliefs that might be unrealistic and unhelpful.

- Gradually facing activities that may have been avoided.

- Trying out new ways of behaving and reacting.

In addition, distraction techniques, mindfulness, and relaxation are also commonly used in cognitive behavioral therapy.

Mood-stabilizing medications are also often combined with therapies to treat conditions like bipolar disorder. The NICE guidelines within the British NHS recognize cognitive behavioral therapy's application in treating schizophrenia in combination with medication and therapy.

Cognitive behavioral therapy usually takes time for patients to effectively implement it into their lives. It usually takes concentrated effort for them to replace a dysfunctional cognitive-affective-behavioral process or habit with a more reasonable and adaptive one, even when they recognize when and where their mental processes go awry. Cognitive behavioral therapy is applied to many different situations, including the following conditions:

* Anxiety disorders (obsessive-compulsive disorder, social phobia or social anxiety, generalized anxiety disorder)

* Mood disorders (clinical depression, major depressive disorder, psychiatric symptoms)

* Insomnia (including being more effective than the drug Zopiclone)

* Severe mental disorders (schizophrenia, bipolar disorder, severe depression)

* Children and adolescents (major depressive disorder, anxiety disorders, trauma and posttraumatic stress disorder symptoms)

* Stuttering (to help them overcome anxiety, avoidance behaviors, and negative thoughts about themselves)

Cognitive behavioral therapy involves teaching a person new skills to overcome dysfunctional emotions, behaviors, and cognitions through a goal-oriented, systematic approach.

There is empirical evidence showing that cognitive behavioral therapy is effective in treating many conditions, including obsessive-compulsive disorder, generalized anxiety disorder, major depressive disorder, schizophrenia, anxiety, and negative thoughts about oneself). With the vast amount of success shown by the use of this therapy, it is one of the most important tools that researchers and therapists have to treat mental disorders today.

Chapter VII

The History of Cognitive Behavioral Therapy

Cognitive behavioral therapy is an approach used by psychotherapists to influence a patient's behaviors and emotions. The key to the approach is in its procedure which must be systematic.

It has been used successfully to treat a variety of disorders including eating disorders, substance abuse, anxiety and personality disorders. It can be used in individual or group therapy sessions and the approach can also be geared towards self help therapy.

Cognitive behavioral therapy is a combination of traditional behavioral therapy and cognitive therapy. They are combined into a treatment that is focused on symptom removal. The effectiveness of the treatment can clearly be judged based on its results. The more it is used, the more it has become recommended.

It is now used as the number one treatment technique for post traumatic stress disorder, obsessive compulsive disorder, depression and bulimia.

Cognitive behavioral therapy first began to be used between 1960 and 1970. It was a gradual process of merging behavioral therapy techniques and cognitive therapy techniques. Behavioral therapy had been around since the 1920's, but cognitive therapy was not introduced until the 1960's.

Almost immediately the benefits of combining it with behavioral therapy techniques were realized. Ivan Pavlov, with his dogs who salivated at the ringing of the dinner bell, was among the most famous of the behavioral research pioneers. Other leaders in the field included John Watson and Clark Hull.

Instead of focusing on analyzing the problem like Freud and the psychoanalysts, cognitive behavioral therapy focused on eliminating the symptoms. The idea being that if you eliminate the symptoms, you have eliminated the problem. This more direct approach was seen as more effective at getting to the problem at hand and helping patients to make progress more quickly.

As a more radical aggressive treatment, behavioral techniques dealt better with more radical problems. The more obvious and clear cut the symptoms were, the easier it was to target them and devise treatments to eliminate them.

Behavioral therapy was not as successful initially with more ambiguous problems such as depression. This realm was better served with cognitive therapy techniques.

In many academic settings, the two therapy techniques were used side by side to compare and contrast the results. It was not long before the advantages of combining the two techniques became clear as a way of taking advantage of the strengths of each.

David Barlow's work on panic disorder treatments provided the first concrete example of the success of the combined strategies.

Cognitive behavioral therapy is difficult to define in a succinct definition because it covers such a broad range of topics and techniques.

It is really an umbrella definition for individual treatments that are specifically tailored to the problems of a specific patient. So the problem dictates the specifics of the treatment, but there are some common themes and techniques. These include having the patient keep a diary of important events and record the feelings and behaviors they had in association with each event. This tool is then used as a basis to analyze and test the patient's ability to evaluate the situation and develop an appropriate emotional response.

Negative emotions and behaviors are identified as well as the evaluations and beliefs that lead to them. An effort is then made to counter these beliefs and evaluations to show that the resulting behaviors are wrong. Negative behaviors are eliminated and the patient is taught a better way to view and react to the situation.

Part of the therapy also includes teaching the patient ways to distract themselves or change their focus from something that is upsetting or a situation that is generating negative behavior.

They learn to focus on something else instead of the negative stimulus, thus eliminating the negative behavior that it would lead to.

The problem is essentially nipped in the bud. For serious psychological disorders like bipolar disorder or schizophrenia, mood stabilizing medications are often prescribed to use in conjunction with these techniques.

The medications give the patient enough of a calming effect to give them the opportunity to examine the situation and make the healthy choice whereas before they could not even pause for rational thought.

Cognitive behavioral therapy has been proven effective for a variety of problems, but it is still a process, not a miracle cure. It takes time to teach patients to understand situations and identify the triggers of their negative behaviors.

Once this step is mastered, it still takes a lot of effort to overcome their first instincts and instead stop and make the right choices. First they learn what they should do, and then they must practice until they can do it.

Chapter VIII

Understanding the Fundamentals of Cognitive Behavior Therapy

Cognitive behavior therapy has been used to help patients who are suffering from depression, anxieties, addictions and all sorts of other psycho social problems.

When under going cognitive behavior therapy a professional helps the suffering person to readjust his or her thinking. It is believed that thinking patterns and the way a person may perceive or relate to certain situations are connected with the patient's emotions and behavior.

Cognitive behavior therapy is a way to help find the underlying causes of the problem from a psychological point of view and then change or correct the thinking pattern that has led to wrong behavior.

Using cognitive behavior therapy, a professional is trying to modify the unrealistic and distorted thinking of the patient. This in turn will help the patient to make changes in behavior and to be able to re-adjust. Thinking patterns and emotions play a key role in human behavior and can be changed or modified.

Cognitive behavior therapy is also used to help people with drug addictions such as cocaine. In the strictest sense of the word, people who turn to drugs, both legal prescription drugs that are addicting, as well as illegal drugs, can be said to have a behavior disorder and can benefit from cognitive behavior therapy.

There are an increasing number of people who are suffering from dysfunctional disorders and while some believe medical treatments may be enough. studies seem to indicate that cognitive behavior therapy is successful. Of course, a lot depends on the person's willingness to comply with a trained therapist and to modify inner thoughts and feelings.

The trained therapist also is helping the patient to understand past experiences and situations, to analyze and to learn not to react in an irrational or distorted way.

Cognitive behavior therapy has become a way of understanding the connection between inner thoughts and perceptions and human behavior. This no doubt has contributed to some success that has been made. It also has helped some people to make big changes in their life.

If you are a person who is suffering from anxiety or depression or any other kind of psycho-social problem, take courage and find a trained therapist in cognitive behavior therapy.

You can learn to make changes in your life and help yourself and those who are close to you. Of course it may take you some time to see a difference in your life, but remember to accomplish anything worthwhile you need determination.

There are also many books written on this subject that you may want to check out. When going online you can also find tons of information that may help you to learn even more about cognitive behavior therapy.

The time you may spend can make the difference. The good news is that, even if you feel overwhelmed and discouraged at times, there is help for you. There is also help in form of seminars that you can attend to learn more about cognitive behavior therapy and how it can help you. Taking time to look over the information available may be your very first step to recovery.

Chapter VIIII

Benefits of Cognitive Behavioural Therapy

Puts patients in control

Medication often works by helping to suppress underlying emotions and thoughts, resulting in the problem never completely being resolved.

Cognitive behavioural therapy, on the other hand, works by helping the patient identify their negative thoughts and emotions while a therapist helps them to better understand how these thoughts and emotions are controlling their actions. Then, the patient is better able to gain control over those thoughts, and the actions that are a result of them.

Not medication

Cognitive behavioural therapy is done completely by talking and acting. While it may be used in combination with medication, it can also be quite effective on its own. In addition to not requiring that a patient take medication, this treatment can help reduce the need for medication in many patients over time, provided they see a therapist on a regular basis.

Effective treatment

Many patients are unsure of whether or not cognitive behavioural therapy will work, particularly in Western cultures that tend to put more emphasis on taking prescription medications. Studies have proven that it can be effective at reducing the symptoms of multiple disorders, including, but not limited to: anger management issues, depression, anxiety, social anxiety, PTSD, sleep disorders and many more.

Long lasting

Because medication does not resolve the underlying issue, the patient often has the disorder that has required that they seek the help of a professional disorder for years. Cognitive behavioural therapy, on the other hand, works by changing the though patterns of the individual, and helps to replace negative thoughts with more positive thoughts.

Because of this, the changes that are made when a patient undergoes cognitive behavioural therapy are often life long, helping to decrease symptoms and guaranteeing that they do not come back.

Better relationships

Often, individuals seek the help of a professional therapist due to addiction or another mental health disorder. This form of treatment helps to decrease bothersome symptoms, and in doing that, it makes the patient more self-aware than ever before.

As patients are able to see how their thoughts affect their actions, and how their actions have an impact on their life as a whole, they are also able to see how their actions affect their relationships.

The end result of this is that many patients experience better relationships in every aspect of their life, including work and home, as treatment progresses and they continue to make progress.

Encourages responsibility

This form of treatment is based on the behavioural model, a model that states that a person's feelings control their thoughts, and then their thoughts control their actions.

Because of this, many individuals wind up accepting the responsibility for their actions instead of blaming other people, situations, or claiming that it is because they are a victim.

While situations are often out of a person's control, how they react to those situations is not, and this is one of the primary beliefs that has helped to shape this form of treatment.

This form of treatment continues to increase in popularity as more individuals are looking for a permanent solution that medication does not provide.

It is often referred to as "talk therapy" because it consists primarily of the patient and therapist talking to uncover feelings and thoughts that control actions.

Talk therapy can help individuals with various mental health disorders and life struggles, and over time can reduce the need for medication.

Chapter X

Counseling and Addiction

Kicking the prescription drug abuse habit -- or any other addiction -- is a major accomplishment. But for most people with opioid addiction, detox is only the beginning of a long-term battle against craving and relapse.

Counseling is an essential part of drug abuse treatment for many people. Cognitive behavioral therapy, family counseling, and other therapy approaches can help people recovering from opioid addiction stay clean. Psychotherapy can also treat the other mental health conditions that often contribute to prescription drug abuse.

Why Counseling Is Important in Addiction Treatment

Opioid addiction is more than a physical dependence on drugs. Even after detox, when physical dependence has resolved, addicts are at high risk for relapse. Psychological and social factors are often powerful stimuli for prescription drug abuse relapse:

* Stress, especially sudden life stresses

* Cues in the environment, like visiting a neighborhood

* Social networks, like spending time with friends who continue to use drugs

These factors can create ongoing, nearly irresistible urges to use drugs. Prescription drug abuse counseling helps addicts escape craving and learn to cope with life, without using drugs.

Several counseling therapies are available for prescription drug abuse, and no one established method is known to be better than another. Likewise, no one approach is appropriate for everyone with opiate addiction. The right drug abuse treatment plan is tailored to a person's addiction and his or her individual needs.

Individual vs. Group Therapy

While any counseling therapy for drug abuse treatment is better than none, group therapy is generally preferred over individual therapy. In group therapy, a person is more likely to be both challenged and supported by peers who are also going through drug rehab. Twelve-step programs such as Narcotics Anonymous are peer support groups that can be a useful part of a recovery program.

Individual therapy can be helpful in the case of a dual diagnosis: coexisting depression, bipolar disorder, or other significant mental health condition that requires treatment in its own right, separate from the opioid addiction.

Outpatient vs. Residential Treatment

Residential therapy separates the addicted person from the environment that allowed him or her to use drugs, and teaches new habits or skills for sober living.

A person goes away to a specialized facility for a period of weeks to months. While highly effective in the short term, there is debate as to whether residential programs lead to longer abstinence from prescription drug abuse than outpatient programs.

Relapse is often higher if someone then goes back to a home environment where opportunities to resume drug use are in easy reach. Residential drug abuse treatment programs are expensive, usually costing tens of thousands of dollars and are not always covered by commercial insurance plans.
Outpatient treatment programs are the usual setting for ongoing prescription drug abuse treatment.

Cognitive Behavioral Therapy

Cognitive behavioral therapy -- or CBT -- teaches a person how to recognize moods, thoughts, and situations that stimulate drug craving. A therapist helps the person avoid these triggers, and replace negative thoughts and feelings with healthier ones that are more consistent with sobriety.

The skills learned in cognitive behavioral therapy can last a lifetime, making it a potentially powerful method of drug abuse treatment. However, not all therapists are trained in cognitive behavioral therapy techniques, which can be complex.

Contingency Management Therapy

In contingency management therapy, a person in drug abuse treatment receives positive incentives for staying clean. Vouchers for goods and services, or privileges in a more rigid treatment setting are common incentives. Contingency management therapy is effective in drug rehab studies. But skeptics point out its high costs, and that when incentives stop, its positive effects decline.

Motivational Interviewing

Traditional therapies for drug abuse treatment involved confrontation. Addicts are masters of denial, the thinking went, and therapy should break down walls to force them to accept the reality of their addiction.

While confrontation may still have a role, many therapists instead promote motivational interviewing, a newer counseling method. In motivational interviewing, a therapist seeks to understand and enhance an addicted person's natural motivation for change.

For example, if the person reveals he is motivated by love of his family, or returning to work, these may become the focus of therapy.

Couples and Family Therapy

Prescription drug abuse and opioid addiction don't only affect the user's life; the whole family is transformed. Strong relationships with family and friends are essential for successful drug abuse treatment. Various counseling methods include the spouse and other family members of the addicted person.

There are several potential benefits of family or couples therapy:

* Family members can act as a powerful force for change in the addicted person's life.

* Including family members can increase the likelihood a person will stay in therapy.

* Each family member can begin to heal the damage their loved one's addiction has caused in their own life.

Studies show family therapy results in lower relapse rates, increased happiness in the family, and better functioning in children of addicted parents.

Maintenance Therapy

Most experts today consider opioid addiction to be a chronic, relapsing illness. Just like other chronic illnesses such as diabetes or high blood pressure, opioid addiction treatment in some form must be lifelong.

Many people with opioid addiction will continue to take maintenance therapy. A form of buprenorphine (Probuphine) is now available as an implant under the skin for preventing a relapse of opioid dependence.

It provides a constant dose of buprenorphine for six months and can be used by people who have completed acute detoxification and are already maintained on a stable dose of oral buprenorphine.

Other medications include methadone, naltrexone (which blocks opiate receptors and prevents opiates from causing a high) or Suboxone (buprenorphine/ naloxone) -- medications that are sometimes taken for many years in order to minimize relapse risk.

By the same token, experts say, they should also continue some form of counseling.

The idea of long-term, open-ended treatment runs counter to the one-time view that a person was likely "cured" in a relatively short time after attending a drug rehab program.

However, evidence is mounting that lifelong treatment with maintenance medication along with counseling or therapy should be standard drug abuse treatment for most people with relapsing opioid addiction.

Chapter XI
Drug Addiction Treatment

Medical professionals have made incredible advances in drug addiction treatment over the last few decades. With recent advances in neuroscience, psychology, and pharmacology, rehab specialists have developed a variety of proven methods for drug addiction treatment. Thousands of addicts all over the country now make lasting recoveries each year.

Evidence-based therapies are the most important treatments at rehab facilities. These therapies have been rigorously tested and mandated by government and private agencies alike.

However, many rehab centers use other treatment methods to bridge the gap between clinical therapy and real-world living. One of the most effective ways of accomplishing this goal is cognitive-behavioral therapy.

Cognitive-behavioral therapy teaches addicts that they can control their emotions with their thoughts. This is crucial during drug addiction treatment, as many substances abusers have control issues which contribute to the development and continuation of their addictions.

Negative emotions often lead to relapse in recovering addicts, and gaining control of these emotions is often critical for managing drug cravings.

Cognitive behavioral therapy involves two distinct phases. During the first phase, addicts make personal discoveries about the mental states, emotional problems, and behavior patterns which led them to use drugs in the first place. They also learn why they abused these drugs, and how they eventually developed their addictions. This knowledge is crucial for developing personalized sobriety strategies which work with patients' specific life circumstances.

For instance, cocaine addicts may discover that they typically use cocaine with friends and acquaintances to relieve their subconscious social anxiety.

Likewise, alcoholics may find that they drink in response to specific stressors at home or in the workplace. Making these kinds of direct connections between emotions and drug use is essential to the success of cognitive- behavioral therapy.

The second phase involves the development of strategies for avoiding addiction triggers and managing drug cravings when they occur. These strategies require that addicts use reason to overcome negative emotions.

For example, the aforementioned cocaine addicts might learn to logically relieve their anxieties by reminding themselves they are in friendly company, and that they don't need to get high to be social.

Alcoholics with stress-related addictions might learn relaxation techniques which allow them to calm themselves and respond rationally to tough situations.

Effective use of these strategies may require the simultaneous treatment of co-occurring mental imbalances - a task often accomplished during individual counseling sessions with addiction specialists.

Overall, cognitive behavioral therapy is an effective method for helping addicts apply what they learn during evidence-based therapies to difficult situations in their everyday lives. This type of therapy requires dedicated effort from patients and clinicians alike, however. Inpatient, outpatient, and partial hospitalization drug addiction treatment plans offer addicts access the chance to work with rehab specialists who will help them develop these strategies for lasting sobriety.

If you or someone you love is struggling with addiction, click the links below to find a treatment center near you. No matter how much you're suffering, a drug addiction treatment program can help you put your life back together.

The simplest way to describe how cognitive behavioral therapy functions is that it helps the addicted individual to understand those personal feelings and thoughts that influence their behavior negatively or positively.

It helps the individual to focus on a very specific problem and is generally short-term in duration. During the addiction treatment and recovery process, the individual learns how to identify (and then change) those destructive and/or disturbing thought patterns that negatively impact their behavior.

The basics of cognitive behavioral therapy

The underlying premise or principle that CBT is based on is that our personal feelings and thoughts play a basic, fundamental role in the way in which we behave either alone or out in society. As an example, consider the individual who spends a lot of time thinking about airplane disasters such as crashes or runway accidents and avoids any type of airline travel.

The primary goal of CBT is that the individual can learn how to take control of dealing with and interpreting certain aspects of their environment even though they cannot control them.

In recent years, cognitive behavioral therapy addicition treatment has become extremely popular with mental health professionals and other treatment specialists.

Additionally, because CBT is a short-term format, it is considerably more affordable than other types of addiction treatment and recovery therapies. It is empirically supported and has a proven track record of effectively helping individuals to overcome behavioral disorders and substance dependencies.

Different approaches to CBT

Mental health professionals typically employ one of three different approaches to cognitive behavioral therapy, including:

* cognitive therapy
* multi-modal therapy
* rational emotive therapy

So as you can see, cognitive behavioral therapies can become very complex depending on the individual and the severity of their addiction or behavioral disorder.

Chapter XII

Cognitive Behavioral Therapy and the Treatment of Addiction

Addiction can take many forms: alcoholism, substance abuse, gambling addiction, etc. The list goes on. The question that needs to be answered is how can these addictions be eliminated? Nowadays, with the technology boom, online meetings for treating addiction is available as well as online counseling, and other forms of treatment.

One of the oldest addiction treatments is the twelve step program developed by the founders of Alcoholics Anonymous. In these modern times however, other treatment programs are being practiced such as the so called Cognitive Behavioral Therapy that a user undergoes if he/she wants to be sober.

Cognitive Behavioral Therapy (CBT) is a member of a branch of psychotherapy that gives importance to how a person thinks.

It follows that what is on the person's mind will greatly affect the actions and the feelings of the individual.

Several programs under the cognitive behavioral therapy include: Rational Living Therapy, Rational Emotive Behavior Therapy, Cognitive Therapy, Rational Behavior Therapy, and Dialectic Behavior Therapy.

CBT is now being applied in treating alcoholism and substance abuse. It works in the following ways:

It is based on the asking questions (Socrates' method)
Emotional response is given importance in Cognitive Behavioral Therapy, wherein the belief that changing the way a user thinks will make that person feel better as well as act better (e.g. if the user thinks of staying clean for a year, then that will be done successfully).

In CBT, the client and the therapist should interact harmoniously and should trust each other for the treatment to be successful

In CBT, users feel that they are in control because they are made to analyze their actions and they would be the ones to make decisions on the steps they would take. In the event that they feel that a mistake was made, it's up to them to correct it.

The most commonly used CBT program that battles addiction is the Rational Emotive Behavioral Therapy (REBT). It focuses on providing solutions to disturbances and problems that are behavioral as well as emotional in nature that aims to lead to a satisfied and happy individual.

REBT applies the A-B-C-model of psychological disturbance and change. This model believes that the things that people believe in are the main reasons why people are disturbed, and should not be blamed on the adversities that are experienced by the alcoholics or drug addicts.

In this model, the users are taught to examine the things they believe in and do the best they can to turn those beliefs into something that would produce positive results.

Take note that REBT is considered to be a brief therapy that is there to solve specific problems. More complex problems require longer therapy.

The REBT therapist aids the user in improving one self through hard work that would also help the person over come trials and obstacles. At the end of the therapy, the user is expected to feel self acceptance as well as the acceptance of life's realities.
It is said that severe alcoholism and addiction problems can be treated with Cognitive Behavioral Therapy. Its structured teaching method aims to improve on the way the patients deal with life. It is also an effective way to improve

on the user's way of thinking in terms of drinking.

Chapter XIII

Kicking the Habit for Good: Cognitive Behavioral Therapy for Smoking

Cigarette Smoking: Facts and Figures

Approximately one billion people worldwide are cigarette smokers, including 1 out of every 5 Americans . Smoking kills more than 5 million people worldwide each year, and is the single most preventable cause of illness and death in the U.S. It is estimated that one third of smokers make an attempt to quit each year, typically without any professional assistance.

Of smokers who quit on their own, fewer than 3% are successful in becoming permanent ex-smokers. Many smokers find it incredibly difficult to kick the habit and often feel discouraged and pessimistic about ever being able to quit for good.

The good news is that there are effective treatments that can greatly enhance your chances of successfully quitting.

CBT Can Help You Quit

It has been shown that cognitive-behavioral therapy (CBT), combined with a smoking cessation medication (such as the nicotine patch, nicotine gum, and Chantix®, for example), is quite effective for smokers who are motivated to quit. CBT is an evidenced-based psychological treatment that focuses on identifying and changing maladaptive thoughts, emotions, and behaviors that trigger, worsen, and/or maintain a range of problems (such as depression, anxiety, addiction, etc.). Because changing your smoking-related behaviors – and restructuring your thoughts related to smoking urges – is essential to quitting, CBT can effectively be applied to smoking cessation.
An intensive CBT program is typically composed of three phases: preparation, quitting, and maintenance (or relapse prevention).

Phase 1: Preparation

Many smokers wanting to quit may feel compelled to do so immediately. However, engaging in a "preparation" phase can significantly improve your ultimate quitting success. During the preparation phase of a CBT smoking cessation program, there are two main goals:

1. Gaining awareness of your smoking behavior. Smoking may feel like an automatic habit, often occurring subconsciously.

In order to be able to change your smoking habits, you must first gain a full awareness of them. By monitoring the time of day you smoke, the situation or environment you are in when you smoke, and moods experienced when smoking, you will start to understand your unique smoking patterns. In addition, you will be able to figure out common triggers for smoking that can be targeted during the quitting phase.

2. Setting a target quit date. It is very important to set a firm quit date at the outset of the treatment program. The quit date is typically set between 2 to 4 weeks after you start treatment in order to give yourself time to prepare for quitting.

Phase 2: Quitting

1. Managing smoking triggers. Once specific cues for smoking have been identified, you will actively break the links between these triggers and smoking in the following ways: by avoiding these triggers, by changing your daily routines, and by substituting activities in place of smoking.

For example, before your quit date you will want to remove all smoking-related paraphernalia such as ashtrays, lighters, and cigarette packs. This will help turn a smoker's home into the home of a nonsmoker, which will reduce the availability of smoking while also reducing the number of triggers for smoking. You may also want to avoid "high-risk" situations for smoking.

For many smokers, this entails avoiding drinking alcohol, going to parties, or socializing with other smokers. It will also be important to change your daily routines in order to break the automatic links between daily activities and smoking.

For example, you may benefit from taking a different route to work, changing the location of your break while at work, or altering your evening wind-down routines.

2) Medication. Pharmacotherapy is an effective option to help reduce nicotine withdrawal symptoms after you quit. One of the strongest predictors of relapse is the intensity of your urge to smoke. Medications, like the nicotine patch, deliver a safe and controlled amount of nicotine to your body so that you can reduce the physical aspects of your addiction while you utilize CBT techniques to address the psychological aspects of the habit.

3. Coping with triggers after quitting. No matter how much you prepare for quitting, you will likely experience smoking-related triggers at some point after you quit.

There are a number of CBT-oriented techniques that help you cope with your urges such as:

1. Restructuring your thinking patterns related to smoking (for example, challenging the belief that smoking is the only activity that relieves stress)

2. Identifying ways to stay busy (boredom is a common trigger to smoke)

3. Increasing physical activity (exercise has been shown to reduce smoking urges and to reduce weight gain associated with quitting

4. Managing negative mood states (stress and other negative mood states increase smoking urges

5. Coming up with alternate activities to keep your hands and mouth active (for example, eating healthy snacks, chewing gum, holding a pen)

6. Relaxation training using breathing-based methods and muscle relaxation techniques

Phase 3: Maintenance

Unfortunately, most smokers who quit eventually resume smoking within several months. Therefore, learning relapse prevention techniques is critical to maintaining your smoking abstinence. One of the most important things to recognize is the difference between a lapse and a relapse.

A lapse is a temporary "slip" or mistake, while a relapse is returning to regular smoking. CBT can help you understand how you evaluate a slip, and help you to learn from these experiences to better prevent them in the future.

Chapter XIIII

Cognitive Behavioral Therapy for Sex Addiction

Sex addiction is any compulsive, sexually motivated behavior that is acted out regardless of any negative consequences that the behavior might have on one's life. The condition began to be addressed as an actual mental health concern in the 1980s, and though there are claims that it is not a valid illness, an addiction to sex can interfere with daily life, and treatment can readily be sought from a mental health professional.

Understanding Sex Addiction

Also known as sexual compulsion or sexual dependency, the condition of being addicted to sex is considered by some to be a form of obsessive-compulsive behavior, as it can dominate a person's life.

Sex addiction is often solely attributed to men, but the condition can affect anyone: It is estimated that between 18 million and 24 million Americans—between 6% and 8% of the population—experience some kind of sexual addiction, and of this number, up to 12% are women.

Sex addiction is generally characterized by a pattern of increasing, repeated sexual behavior, which is often uncontrollable despite that person's intentions and efforts to stop the behavior.

Acting to fulfill one's intense and frequent sexual thoughts and fantasies will often take priority over family, friends, and work. As with any addiction, problematic thoughts and behaviors may be rationalized and the addiction denied, even when the condition develops to such an extent that it causes the loss of intimate relationships, family, friends, or one's career.

Although there is no one factor that is known to cause the addiction, people who have a parent who acted out sexually or who have a history of familial sexual abuse or addiction may be more likely to become addicted to sex.

Sexual acting out may also begin as a form of stress management or a way to cope with emotional pain, but because tolerance grows with sex addiction, as it does with any other addiction, the behavior will generally increase in order to obtain the same level of satisfaction.

Research suggests that the "high" obtained from the release of chemicals produced during sex, such as dopamine, serotonin, and oxytocin, is the same as that obtained from the use of drugs or alcohol and that this can lead to addictive behavior, especially when a propensity to addiction exists.

Common Behaviors/Symptoms of Sex Addiction

Compulsive masturbation (self-stimulation).
Multiple affairs (extramarital affairs).
Multiple or anonymous sexual partners and/or one-night stands.
Consistent use of pornography.
Unsafe sex.
Phone or computer sex (cybersex, sexting).
Prostitution or use of prostitutes.
Exhibitionism.
Extensive dating through personal ads.
Voyeurism (watching others) and/or stalking.
Sexual harassment.

Molestation/rape

Typically, a loss of control over sexual behavior, and negative consequences experienced as a result of the loss of control, indicate a sex addiction. "Normal" sexual behavior is not something that can be defined, as human sexuality can be expressed in numerous ways.

Fantasies or fetishes, even those deemed unusual, are not indicative of sex addiction, nor are frequent sexual thoughts, masturbation, casual sexual encounters, the controlled use of pornography, or any other sexual behavior that is not compulsive.

Keeping one's sexual behavior secret, feeling shame or guilt regarding one's sexual activities, or attempting to change or modify sexual behavior but being unable to do so may also be signs that indicate an addiction.

Therapy for Sex Addiction

Therapy for sex addiction differs from the treatment of other addictions in that complete sobriety is not the goal, as it often is with, for example, drug and alcohol addictions. Instead, goals are established in treatment:

The person in therapy will generally work with the therapist to identify behaviors from which to abstain. In therapy, potential triggers or danger zones that may facilitate addictive behavior can also be identified and a plan to avoid these triggers developed.

Therapy, such as cognitive behavioral therapy (CBT), can also help with the identification of automatic negative thoughts, so that any unwanted thought patterns that contribute to undesirable behaviors can be modified or stopped.

A mental health professional might also assist with the exploration of the sexual history of the person in treatment and examine any patterns and rituals in that person's life that may contribute to the addiction.

If sexual abuse or other neglect was experienced in childhood, the person can also discuss these in therapy, as past abuse may have an influence on current behavior.

When romantic or familial relationships have been affected by sex addiction, family and couples therapy can also be helpful during the recovery process.

If an addiction is severe enough to have an extreme negative effect on one's life, and outpatient treatment is not effective, intensive treatment at an inpatient rehab center may be recommended.

Treating Sex Addiction

In addition to therapy, support groups and accountability circles, where a small group of people help each other stick to recovery goals and sobriety standards, may also help in the treatment of sex addiction.

A 12-step group, where a person is assigned a sponsor who has also experienced addiction and can be met with at any time, has also been shown to be helpful during the process of recovering from sex addiction.

There is no specific drug therapy for sex addiction, but SSRI (selective serotonin reuptake inhibitors) antidepressant medications and mood stabilizers have been found to be effective at reducing some of the urges to engage in addictive behavior. As depression commonly coexists with sex addiction, SSRIs can treat the symptoms of that condition, as well.

In some cases, the sex addiction is treated as obsessive-compulsive behavior (OCD) would be, and medications such as Prozac and Anafranil may be prescribed to curb the compulsions. There is also research that suggests a pre-existing condition such as ADHD, when untreated, may lead to the expression of obsessive sexual behaviors.

Medications that treat ADHD, such as Adderall and Ritalin, may also be prescribed to treat the underlying ADHD. These medications can often help resolve the manifestation of addictive behavior.

Sex Addiction in the Diagnostic and Statistical Manual (DSM)

Sex addiction is not recognized as a diagnosable mental health condition by the American Psychiatric Association's Diagnostic and Statistical Manual (DSM). According to Chester Schmidt, chair of the DSM-IV Sexual Disorder Work Group, there is "no scientific data to support a concept of sexual behavior that is called sex addiction.

It is more like a symptom of other psychological problems like depression, obsessive-compulsive disorder, or bipolar disorder." However, the American Society of Addiction Medicine and the World Health Organization (WHO) both recognize the condition as an addiction.

Because there are no actual criteria listed for diagnosis—only typical behaviors—a "diagnosis" is currently derived through assessment protocols specifically designed for addiction. According to data provided by Patrick Carnes, founder of the

International Institute for Trauma and Addiction Professionals, sex addiction should be treated as any other addiction, and many people who have sex addiction also have co-occurring addictions such as chemical dependency, eating disorders, workaholism, compulsive spending, and gambling, to name a few.

Case Example

Sex addiction as a coping mechanism: Amy, 26, enters therapy, reporting a depressed mood and suicidal thoughts. She tells the therapist that she has not been happy since her boyfriend of four years left her three months earlier, and that in order to combat loneliness, she has been meeting people in bars and having one-night stands nearly every night.

She says that she enjoys the act of sex but that she feels worse after her partner leaves. Amy also tells the therapist that she often becomes very intoxicated and engages in exhibitionistic acts. Though she often regrets the behavior, she finds it difficult to keep herself from repeating her actions, stating that she longs to feel wanted and loved.

In therapy, Amy comes to realize that her sexual activity is helping her to cope with the breakup, which she never fully grieved or got over.

The therapist helps her to realize that it is all right to grieve and feel sadness for the loss of the relationship, but that engaging in risky, promiscuous behavior will not help her to recover from the loss.

Amy makes a goal of abstaining from sexual activity until she begins to date again and decides that she will no longer visit bars on her own, in order to prevent from being triggered to repeat the pattern of one-night stands, and she continues in therapy for depression.

Heroin Addiction Treatment

A number of treatments are available for people with heroin addictions. Many rehab centers use a combination of treatments for the most effective recovery. The goal of these treatments is to restore some normalcy to how people with heroin addiction act and how their brains function. Learn more about these types of heroin addiction treatment below.

Medically Assisted Detox

Science shows that treating heroin addiction with other meds decreases heroin use. It also reduces criminal activity and the spread of infectious disease. Additionally, these drugs suppress some of the symptoms that come with withdrawal, such as cravings, diarrhea, nausea and pain.

However, detox isn't a heroin addiction treatment itself. Instead, it's a first step in the process of getting help. People who are addicted to heroin need to continue their treatment to build on the lessons that begin in detox.

Behavioral Therapies

Therapists rely on many types of behavioral therapy to treat heroin addictions. They may use these during inpatient or outpatient rehab programs. The purpose of these therapies is to help those with heroin addictions avoid temptation and find other means of pleasure. It also makes them consider the risks of relapse.

Twelve-step facilitation therapy is a strategy that many self-help groups use. It involves three main principles, the first of which is accepting that heroin addiction is a disease and isn't in the control of the addict. Another is giving in to a higher power and accepting the support of others. The third is active participation in meetings.

Cognitive behavioral therapy (CBT) is another type of treatment. It aims to change the behaviors and expectations related to using heroin. CBT also aims to increase the coping skills of those addicted so that they can deal with stress better.

Family behavior therapy (FBT) deals with both heroin addiction and co-occurring issues. Some of these problems include child mistreatment, conduct disorders, family conflict, depression and joblessness.

Psychotherapy

Some people who struggle with using heroin receive a dual diagnosis. This type of heroin addiction treatment pairs with behavioral therapies to address psychiatric disorders and symptoms. However, it doesn't work well as standalone care for addiction.

Heroin Addiction Treatment At 1ST Step Behavioral Health

Finding a quality rehab facility for heroin addiction treatment is important for recovery. People who struggle with addiction can get help at 1st Step Behavioral Health. With inpatient and outpatient programs, 1st Step focuses on creating a caring atmosphere. Staff is also

trained to help people with dual diagnosis
for:

* Anxiety
* Bipolar disorder
* Depression
* PTSD

How to Get Off Marijuana

Marijuana withdrawal & the depression
that follows: Overcoming addiction

Marijuana takes a long time to recover
from. A man in recovery from marijuana
addiction spoke at an addiction conference
I attended some years ago.

He said: "It took three years before the
marijuana bubble burst." While it may not
take quite that long in every case, it can
and usually does take longer than
expected. In part this is due to the
complex nature of the drug itself, in part
how long it takes one's brain to be able to
rewire itself, correcting whatever

unfortunate changes the pot managed to make.

Every person is unique in multiple ways, and differences show up in personality, traits, and susceptibility to addiction, meaning how fast you become addicted, and how fast your brain rewires itself post-addiction. In my own practice I've seen it take three years to recover from marijuana, but not always.

Negotiating the rather wild waters of recovery depends upon what damage regular pot used made in your life-your social and economic life, your relationships, your spiritual life if that is important to you.

The next part of recovery—getting over the problems drug use caused in your life—is not physiological per se, it is more dependent upon cognitive and behavioral habits, psychological factors, and therefore more under your direct control in terms of setting things right again, picking up the broken pieces etc.

I have seen people make progress more easily when they are able to get involved in a 12-step recovery program like AA (Alcoholics Anonymous) or NA (Narcotics Anonymous) or if there are meetings close to where they live, MA (Marijuana Anonymous). What going to AA etc. meetings does is provide someone in recovery with a social group that doesn't use drugs—and in this "better living through chemistry" world we live in, that can be helpful.

In the ordinary day in the lives of ordinary people, they may walk into an ordinary store with drugs on prominent display—different strengths, different flavors, different colors, but right out there, our legal drug alcohol.

That's a better living through chemistry culture. So finding people to socialize with, hang out with, people who don't use drugs, is sometimes difficult.

People using drugs ordinarily hang out with others who are using drugs, and recovery can mean the end of a whole social circle for the recovering addict.

So if it is possible you would be wise to find a local AA or NA or MA meeting and go every day, or as often as there are meetings. If that is not possible, try to find another social group that is not based on drinking or drug use. If your drug use isolated you socially, you definitely need to head out to find social groups with whom to interact.

This is so difficult to do while you are depressed, but you can do it slowly but surely. In early recovery paranoid ideas, obsessions, fears, worries are hum-drum, common.

 But these screwy, frightening thoughts so routine for people in early recovery are to be ignored as much as possible, they're unreal, they're wrong, and meaningless.

Another source of support in early recover. Consider hiring a "professional" to go through it with you. This includes psychotherapists, counselors, social workers, or community peer counselors.

Here I'm suggesting you find one person to talk to who knows something about addiction and who also knows something about depression.

In a 12 step program it is advised that people in early recovery get a "sponsor" who serves as that person-in fact, people often recover more quickly when they have both an AA sponsor AND some kind of individual therapist who can support their continuing abstinence as well as their involvement in AA.

An AA sponsor may be afraid of symptoms of depression, so if that's a big part of the picture for you, then definitely find a therapist.

A cognitive-behavioral therapist (CBT) may be helpful, although you might also make good use of a general "talk therapist" who knows cognitive behavioral techniques. CBT and talk therapy that uses techniques from CBT have been empirically studied as treatment for depression, and they have been found effective.

These things really make a difference, both to the course of a depression, and to recovery from drug addiction.

Using an anti-depressant is also an excellent idea—it will help your brain begin to make proteins ("Brain Derived Neurotrophic Factor" or BDNF) that will lead to it producing new neurons in a process known as "neurogenesis ." So getting treated with an antidepressant prescribed by an MD is a wise move.

Ask your doctor to start you on a low dose, and increase your dose very slowly. This will help you avoid what are commonly referred to as "side effects." Stick with the psychopharmacological treatment, and stick with the prescribing physician—whether he/she is an internist or psychiatrist.

Make use of every possible kind of support. Give yourself permission to go all out on this one, you'll never regret it.

Begin a program of meditation right now, today. Currently this is being called "mindfulness" but really, it is good old-fashioned meditation, an activity that's been used to help people with "mind problems" for almost 5000 years.

It is not hard to learn, try it today. Simply sit down somewhere and for three or four minutes, partly shut your eyes (or shut them completely if that is easier) and try to pay attention to your breath, breathing in and breathing out.

You don't have to breathe particularly deeply, just breathe your normal way. You can count each breath with each exhalation. Or you can say silently, to yourself "I's breathing in, I'm breathing out." If three minutes is too long, do it for two minutes.

Eventually you will be able to do it for longer. Don't worry about all the thoughts that come into your mind and drag your attention away from your breath-when you notice them, simply go back to paying attention to your breathing. Being dragged away by thoughts is entirely normal, it's how our minds work.

Bringing our attention back to our breath is the magic, that's the activity that rewires the brain. Doing this for very short periods of time in the beginning is much better than trying to meditate for a longer time that might get uncomfortable. You want to love your time meditating.

Daily meditation will rewire your brain. It will help regulate your emotions. That hyper-sensitivity to negative comments, to feeling rejected, will change. You'll become more resiliant

Start taking walks every day, the longer the better. Any physical activity or exercise you even half enjoy will help you. And exercise has been demonstrated to help rewire your brain more efficiently. Like anti-depressants, it kicks your brain into gear so that it begins making more BDNF.

Educate yourself about addiction disease. There are many books out there about it, many of which are written by recovering addicts just like you. Read their stories, learn about this disease that is as they say in AA "cunning, baffling and powerful."

It is but it can go into complete remission and stay there by the simple method of not using any mind-altering, "recreational" drugs.

A side comment: You mentioned having drug dreams—where marijuana made an appearance. This is normal for people who are withdrawing from drugs. They are "warning dreams," that is in your dream you are telling yourself that you are in danger of using marijuana again.

You're reminding yourself to be cautious, be alert and vigilant and avoid using marijuana. You also mentioned light drinking on occasion. From clinical experience I feel obliged to say that using "other" drugs, or drugs that were not the recovering person's' "drug of choice" is risky.

Drugs often work to drop inhibitions, drugs interfere with decision-making. Using alcohol at all is likely to end up a problem. Being around people who recreate by drinking is a problem, because your recreational drug has been marijuana. As said above, find people who know how to relax and recreate while drug-free. You can do this.
Cut yourself some slack. Whatever "bad" or "stupid" things you did in your addiction are NOT your fault, they are the fault of the disease of addiction. Addiction highjacks the brain. It highjacks the part of the brain responsible for making decisions. It highjacks the pleasure center in the brain.

These problems will be corrected with time off mind-altering drugs (and by this I do not mean antidepressants). What you do now, in your recovery, is your responsibility. But what happened in the past, put that aside.

You will make amends if you need to, later. For now try to dump all the feelings of guilt, all your worries about other people. Try to take these steps I've suggested, even if you are weighed down by depression. The ups and downs of pot withdrawal are difficult, but they will diminish slowly but surely, and you will recover completely.

Tools to Combat Bad Habits After You've Kicked Addiction

Often throughout addiction, you will also pick up some bad habits along the way. Making it past recovery was probably one of the biggest challenges you've ever faced. Now it's time to tend to the bad habits that tagged along.

On one hand, you may want to hold onto your bad habits as it's something familiar.

On the other hand, you know you can kick bad habits because you made it through addiction recovery.

Smoking is one of the major habits that you still hold onto even though you're past substance addiction. It is unlikely that you'll go through addiction treatment and smoking cessation simultaneously. This leaves you still smoking even after you've stopped drinking or using drugs.

Bad habits like smoking, hoarding, eating junk food, or spending too much time online hinder your life experience. They may not always be life threatening but they're not healthy either.

What is a Habit?

Habits are behaviors that occur subconsciously. They are something we do often and they can be good or bad. Brushing your teeth after meals is a good habit.

A bad habit is a patterned behavior that has proven to be detrimental to the physical or mental health of a person. Smoking or overeating are considered bad habits.

The Difference Between a Bad Habit and Addiction

There are similarities between a bad habit and addiction but they do differ. Addiction involves physical and psychological dependency. The habit of drinking when a person needs to cope quickly becomes a tolerance and dependency, making it an addiction.

It takes a few weeks to break a habit but addiction can take months or years to recover from fully. In this regard, addiction is seen as a much more challenging issue than a habit.

Co-occurrence of Substances and Bad Habits

To illustrate this point, we'll use smoking. Smoking is probably the most common bad habits that is picked up for addicts. It is more challenging to get smokers to stop when they're going through alcohol withdrawal.

Compared to other smokers who aren't addicted to substances, they smoke more and higher amounts daily. This increases their dependence. Many smokers who suffer from alcoholism report that they use smoking to cope with alcohol or drug use urges.

1. Deal with Bad Habits one at a Time

Self-affirmation and self-control are what make up your willpower. Ego depletion is a term used to explain that we have a limited amount of willpower available on any given day. When it becomes taxed, it becomes more challenging to control impulses.

If you are trying to deal with too many things at once, you won't be able to deal with temptations. This is why it's important to deal with breaking one bad habit at a time.

Each habit you're trying to change will require willpower, leaving you in a state of glucose depletion. Due to lack of energy, it can cause you to cave in quite easily.

2. Avoid Going Cold Turkey with Your Bad Habits

While going cold turkey might work for some, it's based on the emphasis of perfection. There is a risk that the person could fall off the wagon.

When you quit cold turkey, this equates to absolute failure which causes relapse. There is no mental wiggle-room for the moment you cave into temptation.

This creates a feeling of defeat instead of taking each day at a time, you decide that you might as well binge on your habit.

This causes you to take part in the habit more than you had before.

3. Daily Incremental Improvements

To permanently change and move past a bad habit, you want to focus on daily, incremental improvements. Tapering off to get rid of the habit helps you to succeed. Decrease the amount and the frequency that you do the bad habit.

First, you'll want to define your baseline metric. This will vary based on the bad habit you want to change.

How many cigarettes do you smoke daily?

How many times do you bite your nails in a day?

How much do you weigh right now?

How many calories are you consuming daily?

How much time do you spend online or on social networks?

How much time do you spend watching TV?

4. Retrain the Mind to See Your Bad Habit Differently

There are plenty of habits we do that we can't stand. Biting our nails hurts and smoking tastes terrible and costs a lot of money. We keep on doing them because they provide a sense of satisfaction or a reward to the mind. Instead of glorifying the bad habit, reframe your mind to see things as they really are.
Pay attention to the thoughts that occur when you are craving the bad habit. Ask yourself how you could think differently.

Grow to greatly dislike the habit itself that you've been holding onto and note all of its bad points.

5. Review Your Bad Habit Relapse

Expect to experience relapses and with this anticipation, create a plan in advance to get back on track. See the relapse as a learning experience to help you better understand what happened. This will allow you to avoid it for the next time.

6. Understanding the Habit Loop in Yourself

Your best strategy for long-term success is to identify habit loops. Habit loops are actions that take you from the cue to reward.

When you understand these actions, you'll know how to take steps towards bad habit changes.

You want to slowly replace habits with healthier routines. This way, you won't focus on what's missing in your life. You can find healthy routines that give you the same rewards.

Every habit has the same pattern. They are as follows:

The Cue: This is the situational trigger based on the personal reward you're seeking.
The Reward: The satisfaction you get when you follow the bad habit routine.

The Routine: The physical or emotional action you take to get your reward.

7. Pay Attention to Your Bad Habit Triggers

We are constantly getting cues to take certain actions. The cue can be internal or external based on what one of your senses pick up.

To really change bad habits, you have to understand why triggers happen. To do this, you should record information whenever you feel the desire to commit to your bad habit. The information is as follows:

Location: Where are you?

Time: Write down the time of day where the urge was felt.

Mood: How were you feeling emotionally?

People: Who were you with or what people were around you?

Action: What were you doing at the exact moment the urge surfaced?

8. Make the Changes Based on Bad Habit Trigger Points

Once you begin to see the pattern of where, how, and why your bad habit urges arise, you can make changes. If you find that your triggers are happening every time you're in a certain spot, it's time to stop going to that spot.

This goes for the people you spend time with, keeping your mood in a positive state, and doing certain things that trigger you.
It can also help if you try the 20 second rule. This is where you tell yourself that even though a trigger has occurred, you're going to give it 20 seconds before succumbing to your bad habit.

9. Cognitive Behavioral Therapy

If you're having a hard time recording information or making incremental changes on your own, you might want professional help. Cognitive Behavioral Therapy has been found to be incredibly helpful in complex addictions and mood disorders.

A therapist will help you figure out what your cues are. The habits you have formed are learned so they can be unlearned also.

When you do react differently to your cues, it weakens the habit.

Within CBT, you will break habits with a step by step approach. They include:

* The decision to change

* Use of tools that make you aware of cues

* Devising strategies that assist in stopping the habit

* Being consistent through the process and keeping track of everything involving the bad habit

* Learn to manage your lapses

With addiction and bad habits, you can heal yourself by having more positive interests. First you have to get to the emotional reasons that bad habits began in the first place. You don't need to use substances or habits to cope with negativity in your life.

Instead, you can use strategies to help you cope with whatever trauma comes up in your life. These tools are what will prevent further pain in your life.

Once you do that, you can begin to replace those bad habits with good habits.

Behavioral Treatment For Gambling Addiction

While no actual physical components drive it, a gambling addiction can take hold of a person's life in much the same way as an alcohol or drug addiction. A loss of control over gambling can bleed into work life and relationships just like any other type of addiction.

This leaves the mind and its thinking patterns as the main driving forces behind the addition. Likewise, treatment for gambling addiction relies heavily on behavioral approaches that help a person break the addiction by breaking the thinking patterns that feed it.

A "Process" Addiction

A process addiction is an uncontrollable urge to do something repeatedly in spite of how it affects your social and/or financial well-being. Gambling addictions fit the bill to a tee.

Rather than the combined physical and mental urges brought on by substance abuse addictions, process addictions are behavior-based in terms of the behavior itself as the main driver of the addiction.

Because of this behavioral component, treatment for gambling addiction relies heavily on behavioral therapies. The rush and excitement (or "high") gambling brings works in much the same way as the high experienced from doing drugs. Instead of a physical high driving the addiction, a person's actions and choices set the addiction in motion when it comes to gambling.

Treatment for gambling addiction focuses on replacing the actions and choices that trigger gambling with more productive ones.

Behavior Therapy

As treatment for gambling addiction centers around eliminating destructive gambling behaviors, behavior therapies (based on the classical conditioning model) are a commonly used treatment approach. According to the University of North Texas Libraries resource site, behavior therapy may involve one or more of three different techniques:

* Aversion therapy
* Imaginal desensitization
* In vivo exposure

When used as a treatment for gambling addiction, aversion therapy uses an unpleasant stimulus, such as a small electric shock or loud noise to recondition a person's response to gambling behavior.

Imaginal desensitization involves using relaxation techniques and visualization exercises to change a person's physical response to gambling activities. Like imaginal desensitization, in vivo approaches combine relaxation techniques with the actual experience of gambling to recondition a person's physical response.

Treatment for gambling addiction typically takes place in either individual or group therapy settings as part of a treatment program.

Cognitive Behavioral Therapy

While behavior therapy approaches work directly on a person's gambling behaviors, cognitive behavioral therapy targets the underlying belief systems that fuel a gambling addiction.

As a treatment for gambling addiction, the cognitive behavioral approach seeks to help a person see gambling in a different way. By changing a person's underlying belief system, thoughts and behaviors naturally follow suit.

Cognitive behavioral therapy also addresses other underlying issues that may feed a gambling addiction, such as unresolved problems surrounding a person's self-image, relationships with others and mental health problems.

By working through any unresolved issues, a person has no reason to use gambling as an escape outlet.

As part of a cognitive behavioral treatment for gambling addiction, participants also confront any irrational beliefs they may have about gambling and the actual risks involved.

Since a gambling addiction functions as a behavior-based, process addiction, behavior-based treatments work best when it comes to breaking the addiction's hold on a person's life.

Cognitive Behavioral Therapy for Internet Addiction

Internet addiction, also known as problematic Internet use, is becoming increasingly recognized as a mental health concern. An Internet addiction is typically characterized by a level of Internet use that impairs relationships; brings about family, work, or interpersonal difficulties; and impacts daily function in a negative way.

A qualified therapist or other mental health professional can often help those seeking treatment address and resolve this concern.

Understanding Internet Addiction

Internet addiction first began to be studied in the United States in the mid-1990s, and more recent studies have documented Internet addiction in numerous countries, such as Italy, Pakistan, and the Czech Republic.

In China, Korea, and Taiwan, Internet addiction is considered to be a growing health concern: Studies indicate that up to 30% of the population in these countries may experience problematic Internet use. One in eight American adults are believed to experience Internet addiction. Approximately 70% of those addicted to the Internet are reported to also experience some other form of addiction.

The actual cause of Internet addiction is not known, but potential factors are varied. Some researchers have compared it to other conditions involving addiction, such as compulsive buying.

Those who experience Internet addiction may experience a "high" when using their computers that is similar to the high those who shop compulsively experience when making a purchase.

A genetic component may also make it more likely that some who use the Internet in a problematic way will become addicted to it. Familial and social factors may also play a role, as a person might turn to virtual reality more and more often in order to escape negative situations in everyday life.

As one uses the Internet more frequently and experiences positive feelings and sensations as a result of Internet usage, one may come to depend on the Internet in order to feel good or even normal. Types of Internet addiction may include sexting or cybersex addiction, online gaming addiction, addiction to chat rooms or blog sites, and others. Some individuals may spend all of their time online surfing websites or reading blog entries.

Others may use the Internet to shop compulsively or participate in online gambling, though these, along with sex addiction, are recognized as separate addictions.

In some cases, gender may play a role in the type of addiction one experiences. Research has shown that men may be more likely to become addicted to online games, cybersex or porn, and gambling online, while women may be more likely to use social media, test or quiz websites, and online stores in a problematic manner.

Identifying Internet Addiction

A person who is experiencing Internet addiction may:

* Exhibit a preoccupation with the Internet, even when not using it

* Use the Internet more and more frequently

* Be unable to stop or cut back on Internet use (in spite of attempts to do so)

* Feel moody, irritable, low, or restless as a result of attempts to cut back on Internet use

* Use the Internet to regulate mood or gain relief from the negative effects of problems

* Risk losing employment, romantic relationships, friendships, or academic standing in order to spend more time online

* Lose sleep, experience fatigue, feel apathetic

* Lie to family members, friends, or mental health professionals about Internet use or time spent online

Though one of the characteristics of Internet addiction is the amount of time spent online, what truly factors in the condition is the way the Internet is used and the affect it has on one's life. A person may spend 40 hours a week using the Internet for work and then come home and spend an additional 2-3 hours using the Internet each day.

This practice, however, would not be considered to be addiction unless it had a negative or harmful impact on the individual's life. Further, in the case of problematic Internet use, the amount of time spent online generally increases over time.

The Effects of Problematic Internet Use

Problematic Internet use can be harmful because it often has a significant impact on one's daily life. A person's employment performance or academic standing may fall, and relationships with family members, friends, and romantic partners may be impacted negatively. A person might experience health concerns such as fatigue, headaches, backaches, or carpal tunnel syndrome. Mental health concerns such as eating and food issues, depression, stress, and anxiety may also be associated with Internet addiction.

Late-night log-ins are likely to disrupt sleep patterns and may lead to fatigue, and long-term sleep deprivation is likely to have a negative effect on health.

Additionally, those addicted to the Internet may become isolated as a result of the experienced addiction, though some may have turned to the Internet in order to combat isolation in daily life.

Therapy for Internet Addiction

Currently, Internet addiction is not a diagnosis in the Diagnostic and Statistical Manual. However, it is believed to share similarities with impulse control disorders and gambling addiction.

Internet addiction is believed to be a largely treatable condition. When the addiction is acknowledged, a therapist or other mental health professional can help an individual take steps to address the behavior and regain the ability to use the Internet in a healthy way.

Internet addiction differs from some other types of addiction in that some level of Internet use is generally necessary for function in society. Thus, the goal of treatment is usually not complete abstinence.

However, when a person is addicted to online porn, for example, treatment goals may involve using the Internet without attempting to seek out pornography.

Cognitive behavioral therapy, self-help treatment groups, group therapy, and family therapy have all been shown to be effective methods for the treatment of Internet addiction. Dr. Kimberly Young, who founded The Center for Internet Addiction in 1995, developed a specialized form of cognitive behavioral therapy to treat Internet addiction, CBT-IA.

Twelve-step programs and social skills training may also be treatment options for some individuals. When a mental health concern such as stress, depression, or anxiety has led a person to turn to the Internet for support, a therapist may work to treat the addiction by first addressing this mental health condition.

Similarly, any other underlying conditions are often exposed through work in therapy, and treating these concerns can often help facilitate recovery from the addiction.

In China, a number of "addiction boot camps" have been developed to treat Internet addiction in Chinese youth. However, some young people have died while in these camps, which operate under strict rules and military-style discipline, and a number of these camps have been featured in news stories that have exposed their harmful practices.

In order to help reduce the high number of individuals experiencing Internet addiction, China has developed laws regulating adolescent use of Internet cafes, and the government has made attempts to regulate the number of hours that young people can use the Internet. An inpatient treatment center has also recently been opened in Beijing.

Case Example

Therapy to address teen's Internet use: Momo, 16, comes to therapy with her parents, somewhat reluctantly. She at first resists the therapist's attempts to draw her out while her parents tell the therapist,

"All she does is sit in front of the computer and talk to strangers." They tell the therapist Momo hardly eats, sleeps irregularly, has lost weight, and displays no interest in the outside world. They also express concern for her safety.

Momo displays signs of irritation, and the therapist asks her parents
to step out of the room. Though still resistant, Momo begins to open up slightly in the absence of her parents. The therapist asks her about her life: school. friends, and relationships with family members. After some time, Momo admits that she has been having a difficult time at school.

Her best friend recently became friends with a group of girls who Momo does not find it easy to get along with. The rest of her classmates already belong to close-knit friend groups, and it is difficult for her to join in. She reports small instances of bullying, but tells the therapist she's "lucky" and "others have it worse."

The therapist tells her that no one is "lucky" to be bullied in any amount. Momo eventually reveals to the therapist that she has a number of friends online who are experiencing a situation similar to hers, and she feels as if they are the only ones who understand her. Thus, when she is away from them, she feels lonely and isolated, and so she desires to spend more and more time online.

The therapist normalizes Momo's desire to spend time, virtual or otherwise, with people who understand what she is going through, but helps Momo see it may not be healthy for her to spend quite so much time online.

They attempt to work out a balance between her time online and her time engaging in activities necessary for her life: homework, regular meals, sleep, and other forms of self-care.

In therapy, Momo also begins to address her feelings of isolation and loneliness, and after several weeks, her mood begins to improve, and she finds that she is able to spend time talking to her friends without her Internet time affecting her life. With the help of her parents, she also begins to schedule safe meetings with some of the people she chats to, and spending time "in the real world" with these friends also has a positive effect on her mood.

Chapter XV
Shopping Addiction Treatment

A serious problem with over-shopping is unlikely to go away on its own. Canadian researchers compared substance and behavioral addictions (including compulsive buying) over a five-year span and found that shopping addiction was typically not a short-term problem for those affected.

For about half of excessive shoppers, the compulsive behavior is ongoing, compared to addictive behaviors such as compulsive gambling and video gaming and overeating, which tend to be more episodic.

That means that if you or someone you love is trying to overcome a shopping addiction, you'll likely want to seek help. Although shopping addiction isn't yet considered a bona fide addiction (although there are therapists who'd definitely say it is) you can find the help you need.

Unlike drug addiction or alcoholism, though, a treatment (rehab) facility is unlikely to specialize in compulsive buying. Treatment will likely consist of much the same protocol as other types of behavioral addictions, including gambling, sex, porn, exercise, work and others.

So what's most important to know is that there are many tools to help you or someone you care about get better. No matter which approach you choose, it should be customized to fit your needs and will likely incorporate one or more of these therapies:

Counseling. For most people, working one-on-one with a credentialed therapist is among the most important help you can get in overcoming an addiction, no matter what kind. Cognitive behavioral therapy (CBT) is often used to treat many kinds of addiction, including compulsive shopping. With CBT, your therapist will help you identify and change negative and unhelpful thoughts and feelings about yourself that contribute to the urge to buy.

Therapy should also help you lessen the value placed on extrinsic goals (your appearance and a desire to appear financially successful, for instance) and improve valuing intrinsic goals (feeling good about who you are, having closer ties to family and friends).

Some therapists who specialize in CBT also offer group therapy in which you'll hear from other people struggling with an addiction to shopping.

If you have compulsive buying disorder as well as another addiction (such as an eating disorder or a problem with alcohol for which you're being treated), you should expect that your health care providers will typically treat the other addiction(s) along with your shopping addiction and any other mental health issues. This integrative approach has been shown to be most effective.

Much like people dealing with an addiction to gambling, those who overspend frequently end up in tremendous debt, with unpaid bills, rapidly increasing interest payments and sometimes even legal problems.

If this has happened to you or someone you love, you'll want to seek the guidance of a financial advisor and/or debt counselor to figure out a way to pay back what's owed and/or salvage or rehab a credit score.

He or she can help you develop a budget, set financial goals, put you on a debt-reduction payment plan and recommend ways to thwart overspending in the future, such as cutting up all credit cards, paying only with cash and using self-checkout lanes. Because self-checkout lanes have fewer impulse-buy products and shorter lines, using them helps to cut down on unplanned spending, by 32.1% for women and 16.7% for men, says research.

Medication

Selective serotonin re-uptake inhibitor (SSRI) antidepressants are sometimes given to help people regain control of their impulse to buy. A few small studies have looked at the usefulness of SSRIs to stabilize mood, as well as opioid antagonists such as naltrexone to help control impulsive behavior and the cravings associated with shopping.

To date, there is not enough research to prove that medication is effective in treatment shopping addiction.

Support Groups. Surrounding yourself with the understanding that comes from a community of people who have shared many of the same experiences is tremendously helpful, no matter what kind of addiction you're dealing with.

If you're looking for a 12-step group, you can turn to Debtors Anonymous and Spenders Anonymous; both offer regular meetings where you can share your struggles and help others who are overcoming overspending, too.

Finding the right balance in your sobriety can be easier when you have others who can help you avoid old haunts and feelings of loneliness or anxiety that might lead you back to unhealthy buying habits.

Just like someone in recovery from a technology addiction can't and shouldn't be expected to never touch a computer again, someone with a shopping addiction can't abstain completely from shopping.

After all, we all need to purchase goods and services to meet our basic needs. Instead, through therapy and support group work (typically), the compulsive shopper learns to identify the emotions that trigger a spending spree and the real needs that aren't being met, says Dr. April Benson, an expert in compulsive shopping who runs the NYC-based Stopping Overshopping program.

By identifying emotional triggers, the compulsive shopper can learn to turn to an alternative activity that will fulfill his or her needs, instead of trying to fill up emptiness with shopping bags full of unneeded items.

Through therapy, the over-shopper will also learn ways to help avoid constantly thinking about shopping, cope with cravings and develop strategies that will circumvent overbuying.

As mentioned above, some of these techniques include not shopping alone, using the self-checkout lane and shopping only with cash (leave credit cards and checkbooks at home).

Chapter XVI
Video Game Addiction Treatment

Whether a video gaming addiction is mild, moderate or severe, it's essential to pay attention to the signs and seek help if you notice the problem getting worse over time. Because this disorder is relatively new, scientists tend to treat the disorder similarly to other behavioral or substance use disorders. Current treatment options include:

Rehabilitation: Sometimes the best option for treating a video gaming problem is going to a residential center ("rehab") for a period of time, especially for those who are simply unable to give up their controllers.

Specialized facilities in the U.S., Korea and China offer various levels of care, including digital detox (which helps someone unplug and cope during the withdrawal stage, which can include feeling irritable, anxious and sad). You or your loved one should expect that a rehab program for video gaming will address not only the gaming issue, but also teach the gamer social and life skills.

Counseling: Cognitive Behavioral Therapy (CBT) is the most commonly used therapeutic approach for Internet gaming disorders.

Therapy focuses on questioning and changing negative and unproductive thoughts and beliefs in order to stop the triggers, behavior and underlying emotions that lead to pathological gaming.

Since it's not possible for most of us to avoid the Internet and technology altogether, therapy instead aims to monitor the gamer's use and teach him or her how to use computers in a healthy way and to live in the here and now, rather than in virtual realities. Counseling can also address impulse control issues and any underlying mental health issues.

Prescription Medication: The antidepressant bupropion (brand names: Aplenzin, Budeprion, Buproban, Wellbutrin, Zyban) is sometimes used to treat gaming disorders, much as it's used in treating some substance use disorders: The medication can help reduce cravings for gaming.

There are many more choices when it comes to treating video gaming addiction.

Chapter XVII

Cognitive Behavior Therapy and eating disorders

Cognitive-behavioral therapy, or CBT, is the leading evidence-based treatment for adults with eating disorders and is also adapted for use with younger patients. It is based on the theory that a person's thoughts, emotions, and behaviors are interconnected and can be restructured to support new, healthier thoughts and actions.

Cognitive behavior therapy provides the foundation for individual and group therapies throughout all levels of care at the Center for Eating Disorders.

Structured treatment that focuses on the present and the future.
The cognitive-behavioral model emphasizes the important role that both thoughts (cognitive) and actions (behavioral) can play in maintaining an

eating disorder. Examples of maintaining factors include:

* Cognitive Factors ~ over-evaluation of weight and shape, negative body image, core beliefs about self-worth, negative self- evaluation, perfectionism

* Behavioral Factors ~ weight-control behaviors including dietary restraint, restriction, binge-eating, purging behaviors, self-harm, body checking and body avoidance

Individuals with eating disorders often hold a negative or distorted view of themselves and their bodies. These highly critical thoughts can result in feelings of shame, anxiety or disgust that often trigger weight control behaviors and fuel a cycle of negative self-evaluation. Guided by a therapist, CBT helps the individual to examine which specific factors are maintaining their disorder and to set personalized goals that are addressed throughout the various phases of CBT.

The phases of cognitive behavior therapy

CBT stresses education and skills training that help the patient gain a thorough understanding of themselves and their eating disorder so that healing can occur. Three phases of CBT may unfold over the course of the inpatient, partial hospital and IOP programs, and some or all of them may take place during outpatient therapy.

1. Behavioral Phase: The patient and therapist work together to formulate a plan for stabilizing eating and eliminating symptoms. Because emotions often intensify during this phase of treatment, tools (coping strategies) for managing these feelings are developed and become an important part of the work. CBT includes in-session activities as well as "homework"
so that new behaviors can be practiced.

2. Cognitive Phase: As treatment progresses, cognitive restructuring techniques (e.g., techniques aimed at

recognizing and changing problem thinking patterns) are introduced. Thoughts and beliefs that perpetuate the problems ("I will only be happy if I can lose this weight") are identified and work aimed at developing new perspectives and ideas ("my self-worth doesn't depend on my size or shape") begins. Additionally, during this stage of treatment, broader concerns such as relationship problems, body image, self-esteem problems, and emotion regulation are addressed.

3. Maintenance & Relapse Prevention Phase: The final stage of CBT concentrates on reducing triggers, preventing relapse and maintaining the progress that's been made. Even though CBT is focused on the elimination of symptoms, the overall goal of the treatment is to assist the patient in making their return to a healthy and fulfilling life. So, very often, once symptoms are stabilized, treatment will expand to include other areas of concern and conflict that can help individuals move towards holistic healing and emotional well-being.

Conclusion

The concept of cognitive behavioral therapy is how we think influences how we feel and how we feel influences how we behave and how we behave influences how we live our lives and the choices we make. Sometimes people just want to make a change in their lives so they seek cognitive behavioral therapy. And one of the ways therapist can help you is that they make you think about different thought processes and your irrational beliefs that you are disputing. CBT teach the clients how to be assertive and more importantly the difference between being assertive and being aggressive. Focus therapy emphasizes changing negative thoughts and maladaptive beliefs so it changes negative thoughts into more positive and reality-based thoughts. If we can change our thoughts we can change our behavior. CBT therapists won't dismiss someone's beliefs but they try and work with them to change their way of thinking that are more beneficial to them. CBT treatment does work and if you need help coping with intolerable events, apply the concepts you learned in this book. You should already have a better understanding of what CBT is about. Your anxiety and stress is only a few sessions away.

Best of luck!